Introduction

Ice hockey is probably the roughest of all sports.

It is easy to get hurt by a razor-sharp blade, a flying stick, or a hard body check.

To Brad Park, the tough defenseman who leads the New York Rangers hockey team, the dangers are worth it.

Brad's fast skating and skill with the hockey stick—together with his fighting spirit—have helped to make the New York Rangers one of the top teams in pro hockey.

SHER-WOOD
PMP

Brad Park

S. H. Burchard

Illustrated with photographs
and with drawings by Paul Frame

Harcourt Brace Jovanovich
New York and London

PHOTO CREDITS
New York Rangers, p. 2.
Brad Park, pp. 6, 9, 10, 16.
Robert L. Cornes, p. 20.
Donald Young, p. 23.
Graphic Artists, p. 26.
United Press International, pp. 29, 31, 32, 36, 38, 40, 42–43, 44, 47, 52, 55, 56, 61.
Dan Baliotti, cover, pp. 34, 51, 58, 63.

Frontispiece: The star defenseman of the New York Rangers, Brad Park

Printed in the United States of America

First edition

B C D E F G H I J K

Library of Congress Cataloging in Publication Data

Burchard, S H
Sports star, Brad Park.

SUMMARY: A simple biography of Brad Park, defenseman for the New York Rangers hockey team.
1. Park, Brad—Juvenile literature. 2. Hockey—Juvenile literature. [1. Park, Brad. 2. Hockey—Biography] I. Title.
GV848.5.P3B87 796.9′62′0924 [B] [92] 75-11778
ISBN 0-15-277998-1
ISBN 0-15-684821-X (pbk)

Contents

Brad may be frowning because he is too little to put on skates.

1

Hockey at the Age of Five

Brad Park started playing ice hockey when he was five years old.
He played with his older brother Ron.
Their parents, Bob and Betty Park, did all they could to help their sons become fine hockey players.

The Park front lawn in Toronto, Canada, was flooded all winter to make a hockey rink.

The boys spent all of their spare time skating.

Betty Park had to get used to the loud thump of flying pucks bouncing off shingles, steps, and garage doors.

"There are more dents in our house than nails," she said.

Bob Park was a coach and referee on boys' hockey teams.

Both parents gave the children advice on how to play.

Ron and Brad before they were old enough to put dents in the side of the Park house with fast-flying hockey pucks

Ron was seven years old when he played on his first team.
Mr. Park was the coach.
"I want to play, too!" Brad begged his father.
"I can skate as well as Ron."
"You are too young," said Mr. Park.

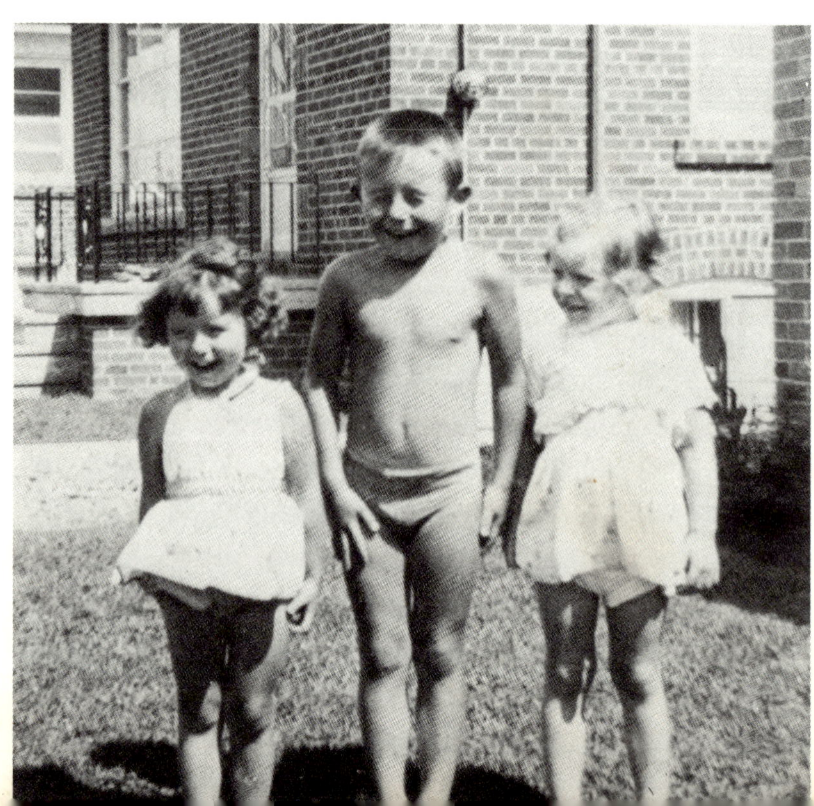

Brad went to all his brother's games and sat on the sidelines.

One day he got his big chance.

The regular goaltender did not come to the game.

Brad jumped over the fence onto the rink.

"I'm a goaltender!" he shouted.

He did not know much about playing goal, but he was willing to do anything to play.

"All right," said Mr. Park.

Brad quickly put on his skates and pads and stood in front of the goal net.

While his brother was off playing hockey, Brad had to stay home and play with younger children.

A big boy skated very fast toward Brad.
He was carrying the puck on his stick.
Brad got scared.
He hugged the right goalpost.
The puck went shooting by into the net for a score.
Brad started to cry.

His mother was nearby.
"Why are you crying?" asked Mrs. Park.
"That guy's not supposed to shoot it in there!" Brad wailed.
But then he wiped away his tears.
He played three more games and did not let himself get scared again.
He even tried a sure way to protect his goal.
When the puck came sliding at him, he would lie down in front of the net to block the shot.

He got wet and cold, but he kept the other teams from scoring.

When the regular goaltender came back, the other boys let Brad stay on the team.

Brad was little, but he was tough.

Besides, he was a fine skater.

The Park family dressed up for a party

2

Moving Up the Hockey Ladder

Brad and Ron soon became the best players on the team.
They could race up and down the ice passing the puck to each other.
They played the game almost by themselves.
No one could take the puck away from the fast-skating Park brothers.

Finally they were asked to leave the league.

They had become too good.

After that Brad and Ron played in the Atom League, where their teammates were better players.

The boys in the Atom League were seven to nine years old.

Brad was only seven when he was made a captain of the team.

When he was nine, Brad moved up to the Peewee League.

Mr. Park was the team coach.

Having their father as a coach was not easy for Brad and Ron.

Mr. Park was strict.

He got angry if his sons made mistakes.

He made sure they were fast skaters, could handle the puck well, and knew how to check.

Brad was one of the two defensemen.

An early team photo. Can you find Brad Park?

One of the most important jobs of a defenseman is checking other players to keep them from getting the puck or scoring.

Checking is a hockey word that means bumping into another player hard enough to knock him down or at least take him out of the play.

It is one of the things that makes hockey such a rough sport.

Brad wanted to play well and please his father, but he had a problem.

He was the smallest member of the team.
It was hard for him to knock the big boys down.
But finally Brad found a way.
It he could not bump them down, he fell in front of them and made them trip over him.

For several years Brad and Ron played on teams coached by their father.

Mr. Park's team was so good one year that it won the Peewee Championship of Canada.

The Peewee champions of Canada

The boys were teammates, but they were fierce competitors. By the time they were in high school, Brad could outskate his brother.

When Brad was seventeen years old, he was asked to play for the Toronto Marlboros, a Junior A team.
Brad was very excited.
Playing on a Junior A team was one step away from being a pro.

Junior A champion Brad Park with team trophies

3

Playing for the New York Rangers

Brad played Junior A hockey
for three years.
Then the New York Rangers
made him an offer.
Brad accepted.
He had a fine rookie year.
He had an even better second
year.
But Brad's third season, 1970
to 1971, was the most
exciting of all.

Coach Emile "The Cat" Francis had turned the Rangers into what looked like a winning team.
The season started badly for Brad.
He asked for a high salary because he knew he was one of the best defensemen in pro hockey.
The Ranger club thought Brad wanted too much money.
After much arguing Brad got angry and left the team.
He went home to Toronto.
Day after day he played cards all by himself.

Business manager and head coach of the New York Rangers, Emile "The Cat" Francis

He was bored and missed the team.
All he wanted to do was play hockey.
Finally the Rangers offered him more money.

Brad returned happily to the Ranger training camp.
He was out of shape for the first game.
He had missed too much practice.
His legs were so stiff that they felt like cement blocks.
He got tired quickly.
But Brad practiced hard.
Soon he was as good as ever.
The whole Ranger team was good.
All season long they battled the mighty Boston Bruins for first place.

Brad fights for the puck with his biggest hockey rival, Bruins' star Bobby Orr.

The Bruins were the biggest and roughest team in pro hockey.

The Boston and New York teams had been rivals for a long time.

Every time the Bruins and
Rangers played, there were
many fights.
Brad had his front teeth
knocked out.

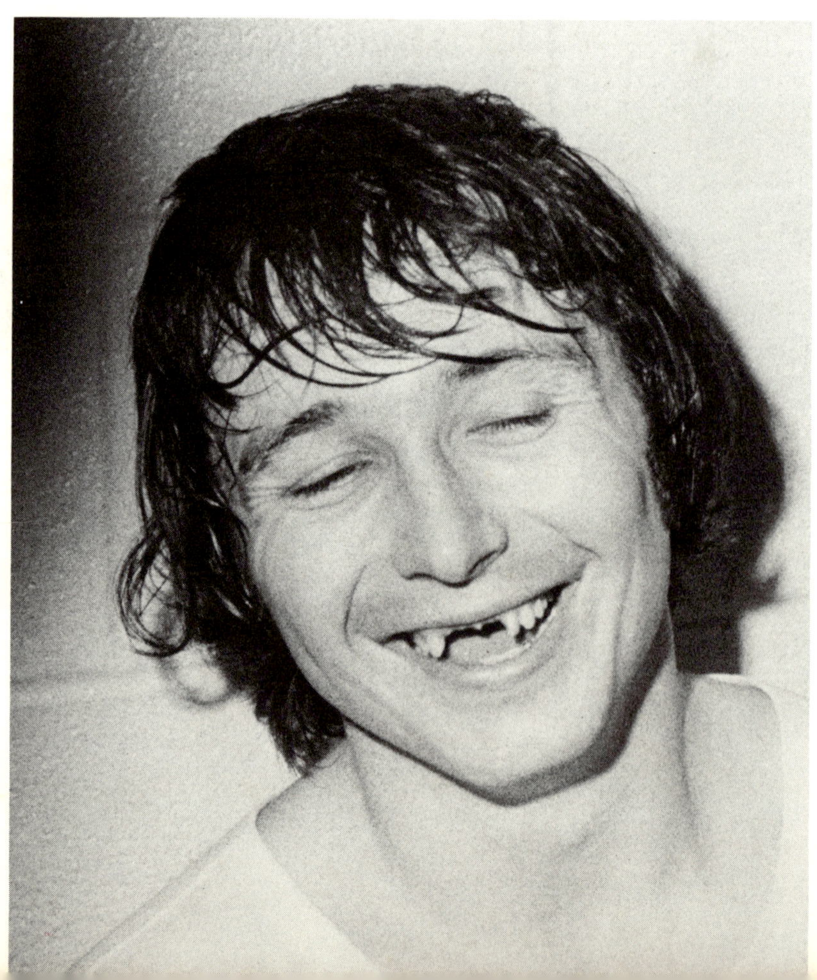

He did not mind when he was knocked down by a fair body check.
That was part of the game.
But if someone hit him too hard or rammed into him on purpose, Brad saw red.
He would take off his gloves and start punching the player who had hurt him.
Sometimes his teammates would skate over to help.
Then there would be a war on the ice.
The referees had to break up the battle.

Like most hockey players, Brad Park had his front teeth knocked out.

RANGER
9

The players who started the fight would have to sit in the penalty boxes for several minutes.

Emile Francis taught his team to play an almost perfect game.

Brad liked the Rangers' style of playing.

He felt they won games by playing well rather than by beating up their opponents.

The whole team worked together.

Brad and the Rangers had a great year, but it was not quite good enough.

When Brad gets mad enough, he takes off his gloves and starts punching.

NHL

The Boston Bruins took first place in their division.
The New York Rangers came in second.

Brad is led away by the referee after his shirt is torn off in a fight.

4

The Stanley Cup

After the regular hockey season
the top two teams from the
four different hockey
divisions play each other
in a series of games known
as the Stanley Cup.
There are three rounds of
Stanley Cup play.
A team has to win four games
to go on to the next round.

Fast-skating Ranger star, Brad Park

The winner is the World
Champion team.
Winning the Stanley Cup is the
dream of all hockey players
and their coaches.

More than anything else in the world, Emile Francis wanted a Stanley Cup win for his team in the spring of 1971.
The Rangers had not won the cup since 1940.
They had not even played in the Stanley Cup series since 1950.
The other New York teams—the Yankees, the Giants, the Jets, the Mets, and the Knicks—had been World Champions in recent years.
The Rangers felt it was their turn.

Park goes for the puck.

They won their first Stanley Cup round by beating the

A pileup of bodies at the Ranger goal during the Stanley Cup play-offs. Ranger forward Jean Ratelle (No. 19) tries to score. Maple Leafs' goalie Bernie Parent falls to the ice to stop the puck from entering the net. Another Maple Leaf skater slams into Brad Park, trying to knock him down. The Rangers won the series.

Toronto Maple Leafs in six games.

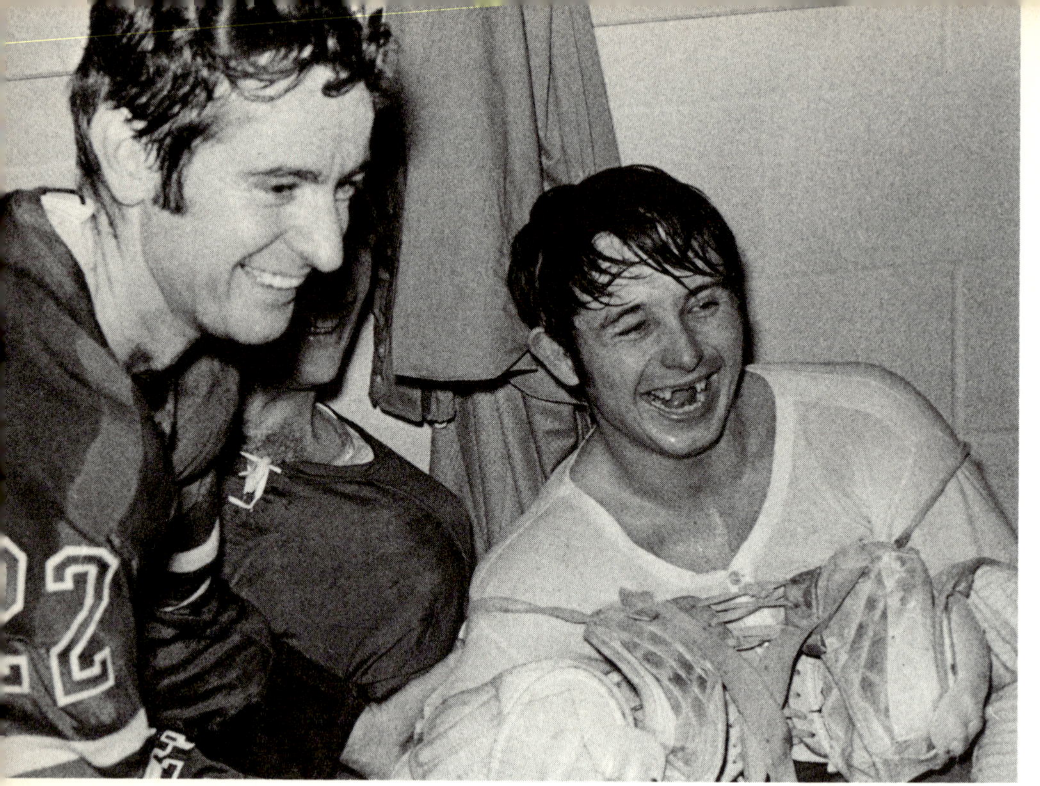

Brad has a good laugh as he and teammates celebrate winning the first round of the Stanley Cup play-offs.

Feeling very happy, the New York team flew to Chicago to begin the second round with the Chicago Black Hawks.

The games were hard-fought and close.
At the end of six games the series was tied three games to three.
The team that won the seventh game would win the round.
Brad had trouble going to sleep the night before the game.
He tossed and turned for hours.
Different ways to play the game kept spinning around in his head.
When the game started, Brad was so nervous that his legs wobbled.

He felt better as he skated around and got used to the ice.

He was sure his team would win.

As the last period started, the score was tied 2 to 2.

"That's O.K.," said Brad to himself.

"They can't beat us."

All during the final period the Rangers played a perfect game.

Time after time Brad bumped into the Chicago players to slow them down with hard body checks.

Chicago Black Hawks' star Bobby Hull (No. 9) tries to slap the puck as Rangers Brad Park and Dave Balon try to stop him.

When the puck got too near the Ranger goal, it was usually Brad who snatched it away and passed it up the ice to the waiting New York forwards.

Then it happened.
Brad had the puck near the center line.
He fired it deep into Chicago's side of the rink.
The referee blew his whistle.
He called an icing penalty against Brad.
Icing is the penalty called when a player shoots the puck the length of the ice rink without any other player touching it.
There would have to be a faceoff dangerously near the Ranger goal.

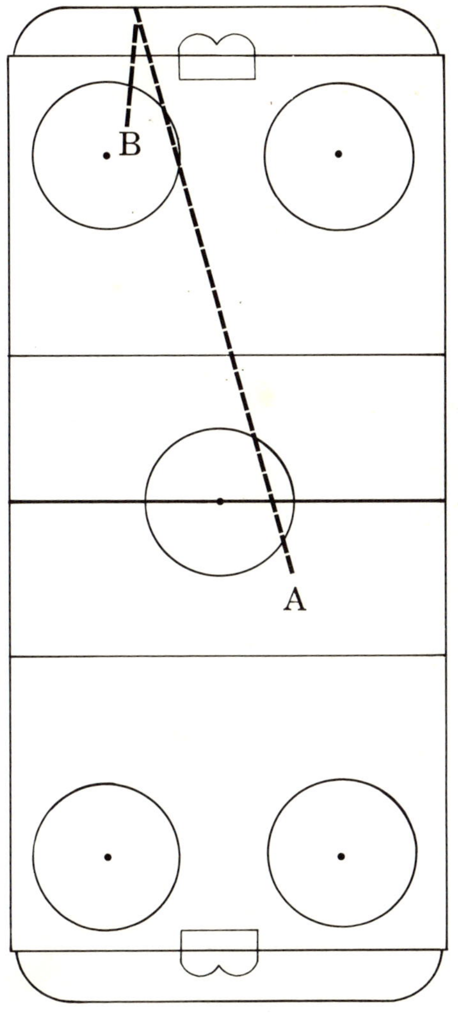

Goal Line

Blue Line

Center Line

Icing takes place when player A shoots the puck from his own half of the ice, past the goal line of the opposing team. If player B (from the other team) is the first to touch the puck, "Icing the Puck" is called by the referee.

The players lined up around the faceoff circle.
The referee dropped the puck.
The Hawks won the faceoff and passed the puck to Bobby Hull.
Hull swung his stick like lightning.
The puck was in the net in a flash, and Chicago went ahead 3 to 2.
Brad and the Rangers kept fighting, but they could not score again.
The Rangers lost by a score of 3 to 2.

A tired and sad Brad Park sits alone in the locker room after losing the chance to win the Stanley Cup.

Back in the locker room, Brad sat on a bench for twenty minutes just staring at the floor.

5

The Rangers Try Again

The Rangers were better than ever the following season.
Again they got into the Stanley Cup play-offs.
This time they won the first two rounds.
In the final round they met their long-time enemy, the Boston Bruins.
The Bruins won the first two games of the series.

Brad Park makes a face as he is slammed up against the side of the rink by the Bruins' Ted Green (No. 6) during the Stanley Cup play-offs.

Brad Park broke the winning streak during the third game played in New York at Madison Square Garden.

Because hockey is such a fast and violent game, the fans often get out of control with the excitement of the play.

On the night of the third game, the New York fans were even wilder than usual.

To show their dislike for the Boston team, they hurled flashlight batteries, cigarette lighters, beer cans, rolls of pink toilet paper, and bags of nuts at the Boston players.

Brad and big Boston center Phil Esposito battle for the puck.

NORTHLAND

"Very tasty," said Boston goalie Gerry Cheevers as he got hit in the back of the neck with a bag of cashew nuts.

In spite of the flying missiles, Brad played his finest game.

He scored two goals himself, and he set up teammate Rod Gilbert for a third.

"Park's two goal shots traveled so fast, they smoked," said a teammate.

"Nobody stops that kind."

Brad led his team to a 5 to 2 victory.

But Brad could not get his team moving again.

The Bruins won the next two games and were Stanley Cup Champions.

Brad Park holds back the Bruins' Derek Sanderson as teammate Dave Balon (No. 17) skates off with the puck.

6

A Tough Year

The 1973–1974 hockey season
was a tough one for Brad.
His two-month-old son, Robby,
got sick with pneumonia.
It was very hard for him to
breathe, and he was in the
hospital for a long time
fighting for his life.
Brad's other son, James, who
was only eighteen months
old, also got sick.

The 1973-1974 season was tough for the Park family, but Brad still enjoyed many happy moments playing hockey.

Both boys finally got better, but it was difficult for Brad to be away from home playing hockey when he was worried about his family.
In front of the other Ranger players Brad was always cheerful.
He played as hard as ever.
"It had to be hard on him," said teammate Ted Irvine.
"But he's a super guy."
Once again, the Rangers made it into the Stanley Cup play-offs.
In the second round they met the Philadelphia Flyers.

Dave Schultz shoves Brad into a corner.

In the third game the roughest player on the Flyers, Dave Schultz, went after Brad. First he shoved Brad into a corner.

As Brad skated back on the ice,
Schultz rammed into him
again and knocked him down.
The fall almost knocked Brad
out.
As he lay on the ice, Schultz
stood over him and began
punching him in the face.
Brad's teammates had to come
to his rescue.
The Flyers had a simple plan.
If they beat up the best Ranger
player, they would win the
series.
The Flyers could not stop Brad
Park, but they did win the
series four games to three.

Brad gets back on his feet after being beaten up by Dave Schultz. Blood stains his uniform.

"Of course I'm upset about losing," said a very angry Brad Park after the last game.
"But I'd rather lose with these guys than win with any others."
Brad is very proud of playing with the New York Rangers.
He is sure that one day they will win the Stanley Cup.